EASY POP *Duets*

7 GREAT ARRANGEMENTS

BY GLENDA AUSTIN, ERIC BAUMGARTNER AND CAROLYN MILLER

INCLUDES ONLINE AUDIO

The online audio tracks give you the flexibility to rehearse or perform these piano duets anytime and anywhere. Each piece features a Secondo part, a Primo part, and a demo track of both parts together that can be downloaded or streamed. The *Playback+* feature allows you to change the tempo without altering the pitch!

PLAYBACK+
Speed • Pitch • Balance • Loop

To access audio visit:
www.halleonard.com/mylibrary

Enter Code
2473-8341-8681-4617

ISBN 978-1-4950-2130-5

WILLIS MUSIC

EXCLUSIVELY DISTRIBUTED BY

HAL•LEONARD®
CORPORATION

7777 W. BLUEMOUND RD. P.O. BOX 13819 MILWAUKEE, WI 53213

Visit Hal Leonard Online at
www.halleonard.com

T0056130

CONTENTS

Bad Romance

SECONDO

Words and Music by Stefani Germanotta
and Nadir Khayat
Arranged by Glenda Austin

Steady Techno beat

* *Add octave above for more intensity.*

Bad Romance

PRIMO

Words and Music by Stefani Germanotta
and Nadir Khayat
Arranged by Glenda Austin

Steady Techno beat

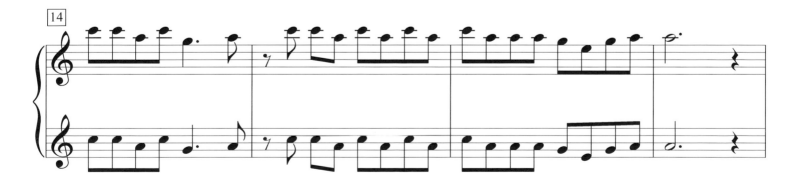

SECONDO

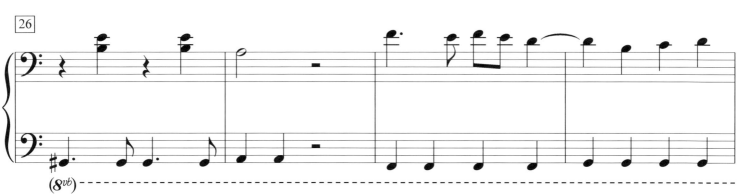

PRIMO

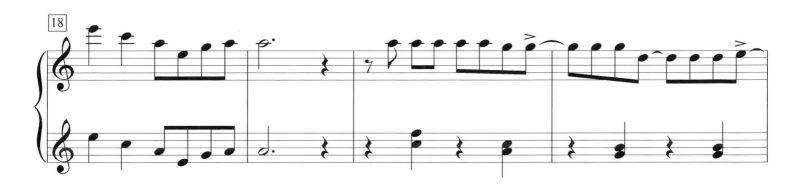

Can You Feel the Love Tonight

from Walt Disney Pictures' THE LION KING

SECONDO

Music by Elton John
Lyrics by Tim Rice
Arranged by Eric Baumgartner

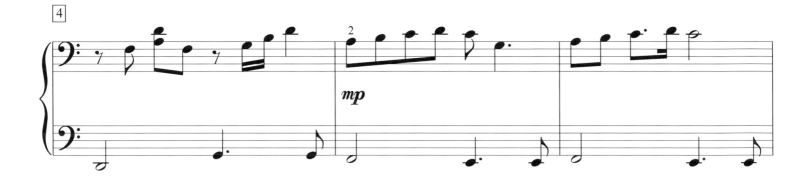

Can You Feel the Love Tonight

from Walt Disney Pictures' THE LION KING

PRIMO

Music by Elton John
Lyrics by Tim Rice
Arranged by Eric Baumgartner

SECONDO

PRIMO

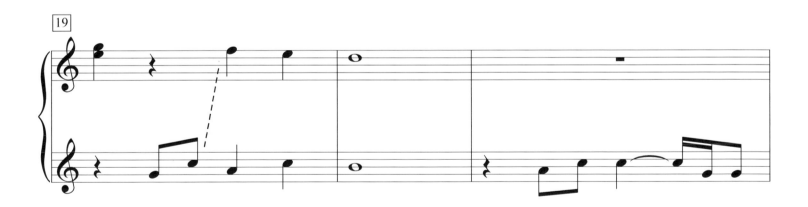

Love Story

SECONDO

Words and Music by Taylor Swift
Arranged by Glenda Austin

Gently flowing

Love Story

PRIMO

Words and Music by Taylor Swift
Arranged by Glenda Austin

Gently flowing

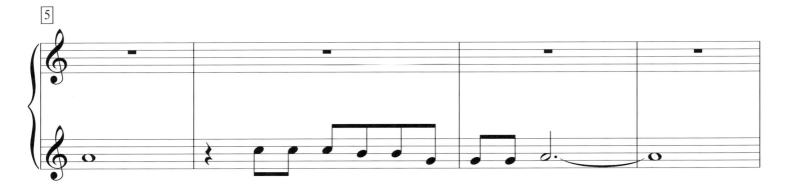

SECONDO

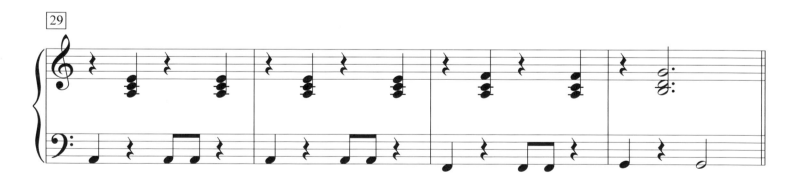

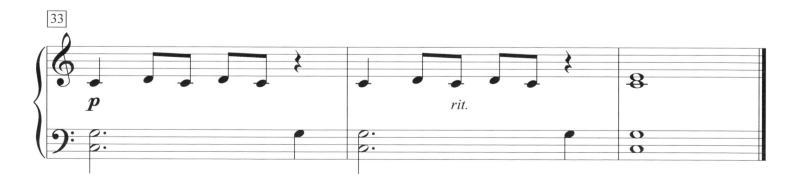

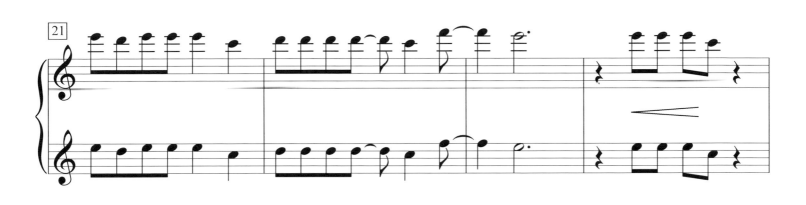

My Heart Will Go On

(Love Theme from 'Titanic')

from the Paramount and Twentieth Century Fox Motion Picture TITANIC

SECONDO

Music by James Horner
Lyric by Will Jennings
Arranged by Carolyn Miller

My Heart Will Go On
(Love Theme from 'Titanic')
from the Paramount and Twentieth Century Fox Motion Picture TITANIC

PRIMO

Music by James Horner
Lyric by Will Jennings
Arranged by Carolyn Miller

SECONDO

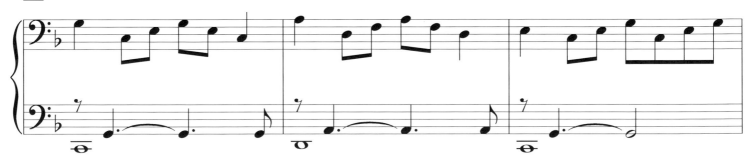

PRIMO

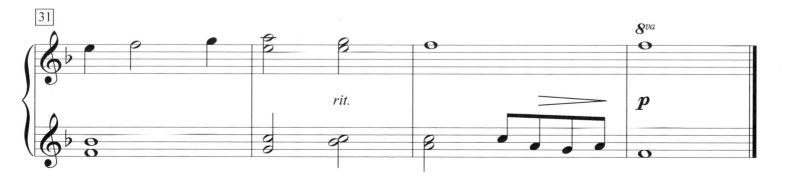

Paradise

SECONDO

Words and Music by Guy Berryman, Jon Buckland,
Will Champion, Chris Martin and Brian Eno
Arranged by Carolyn Miller

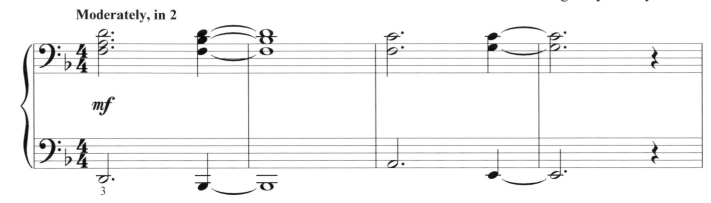

Paradise

PRIMO

Words and Music by Guy Berryman, Jon Buckland,
Will Champion, Chris Martin and Brian Eno
Arranged by Carolyn Miller

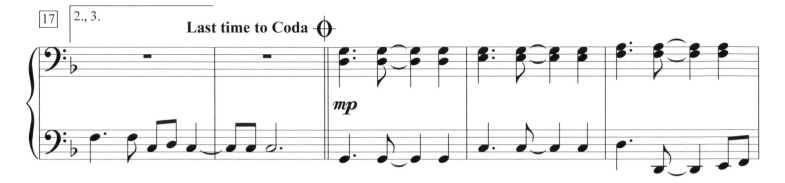

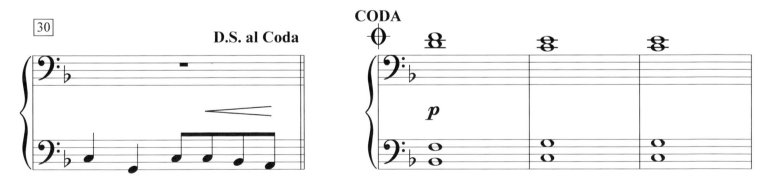

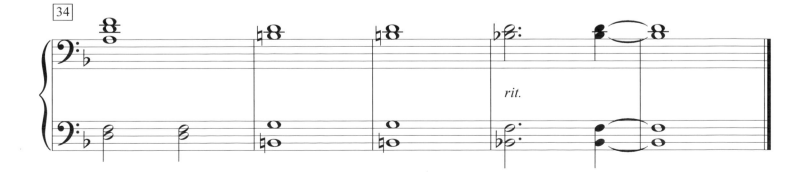

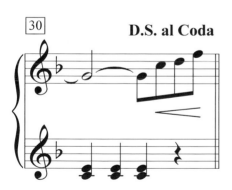

Tears in Heaven

SECONDO

Words and Music by Eric Clapton
and Will Jennings
Arranged by Eric Baumgartner

Tears in Heaven

PRIMO

Words and Music by Eric Clapton
and Will Jennings
Arranged by Eric Baumgartner

SECONDO

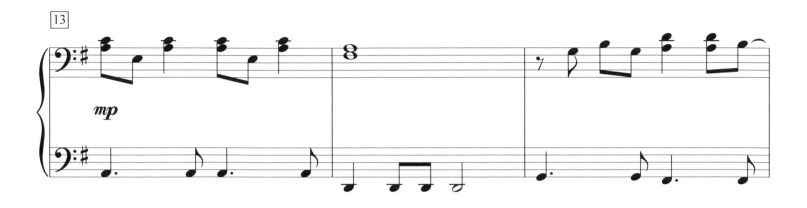

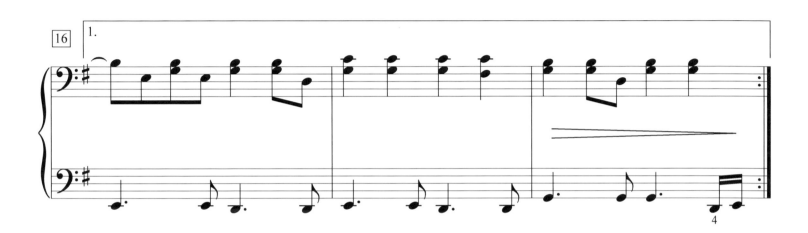

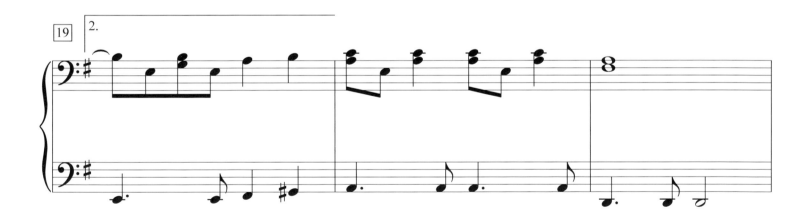

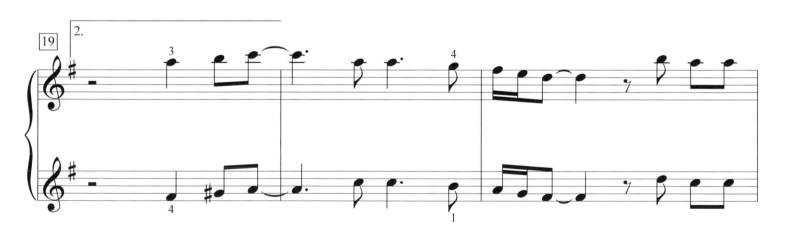

Yesterday

SECONDO

Words and Music by John Lennon
and Paul McCartney
Arranged by Eric Baumgartner

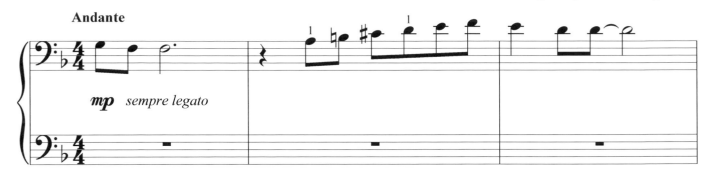

mp   *sempre legato*

With light pedal

p

Yesterday

PRIMO

Words and Music by John Lennon
and Paul McCartney
Arranged by Eric Baumgartner

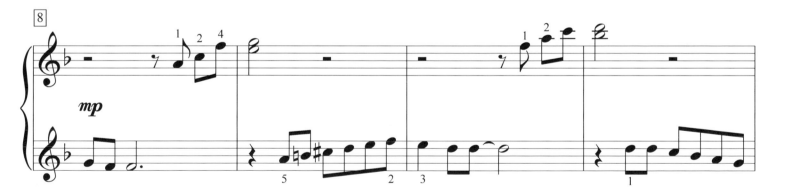

SECONDO

PRIMO

Glenda Austin is a composer, arranger, pianist, and teacher from Joplin, Missouri. A graduate of the University of Missouri, Glenda teaches music in elementary and high school, and is an adjunct faculty member at Missouri Southern State University. She is a frequent adjudicator and clinician for Willis and Hal Leonard, presenting piano workshops for teachers and students throughout the United States, as well as in Canada and Japan. Several of Glenda's compositions appear on state repertoire lists, and two best-sellers, "Jazz Suite No. 2" and "Sea Nocturne," are perennial favorites on the National Federation list.

Eric Baumgartner received jazz degrees from Berklee College of Music in Boston and DePaul University in Chicago. He is the author and creator of the *Jazzabilities* and *Jazz Connection* series, a related set of beginning jazz piano books. Besides composing and maintaining a teaching studio, Eric works extensively in musical theatre and plays keyboard and guitar with several pop and jazz groups. He is the orchestrator of several noted Willis publications, including the *Teaching Little Fingers to Play* series, *Popular Piano Solos,* and his own *Jazz It Up!* series. His wide range of musical influences is reflected in his balanced approach to teaching: he finds validity in all music and works with students to help them find their own musical identity through improvising, arranging, and composing. Eric has presented his unique teaching techniques in the United States, England, and Australia.

Carolyn Miller holds a bachelor's degree from the College Conservatory of Music at the University of Cincinnati and a master's degree in elementary education from Xavier University. A lifelong educator, Carolyn has taught piano to students of all ages, privately and in the classroom, and continues to maintain a piano studio in her Cincinnati home. She presents workshops throughout the United States and is often asked to adjudicate at music festivals and competitions. Carolyn's music often teaches essential technical skills, yet is fun to play, making it appealing to children and adults and resulting in frequent appearances on the National Federation list. In fact, well-known personality Regis Philbin performed two of her compositions, "Rolling River" and "Fireflies," live on national television.